Meditations Journal

Meditations Journal

MARCUS AURELIUS

Clarkson Potter/Publishers
New York

Give yourself a gift: the present moment.

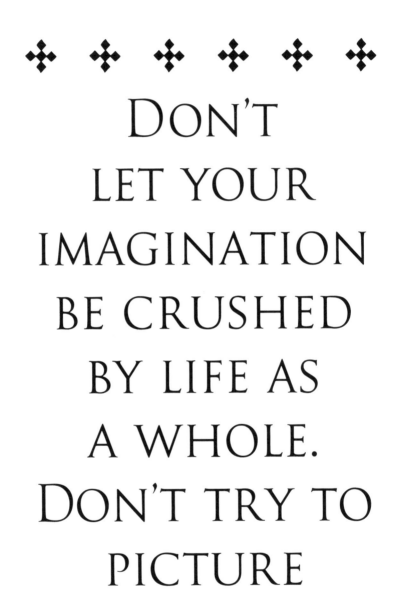

DON'T
LET YOUR
IMAGINATION
BE CRUSHED
BY LIFE AS
A WHOLE.
DON'T TRY TO
PICTURE

EVERYTHING
BAD THAT
COULD
POSSIBLY
HAPPEN.
STICK WITH
THE SITUATION
AT HAND.

✤ ✤ ✤ ✤ ✤ ✤

It's all in how
you perceive it.
You're in control.

Remember—
your responsibilities can
be broken down into
individual parts as well.
Concentrate on those,
and finish the job
methodically—without
getting stirred up or
meeting anger with anger.

Do external things distract you? Then make time for yourself to learn something worthwhile; stop letting yourself be pulled in all directions.

Ignoring what goes on
in other people's souls—
no one ever came to
grief that way. But if
you won't keep track
of what your *own* soul's
doing, how can you
not be unhappy?

How the mind conducts itself. It all depends on that.

All the rest is within its power, or beyond its control.

✤ ✤ ✤ ✤ ✤ ✤

LOOK INWARD.
DON'T LET THE
TRUE NATURE

OR VALUE
OF ANYTHING
ELUDE YOU.

❖ ❖ ❖ ❖ ❖ ❖

It's time you
realized that you
have something
in you more
powerful and
miraculous than
the things that
affect you and
make you dance
like a puppet.

Don't be ashamed
to need help.
Like a soldier
storming a
wall, you have
a mission to
accomplish. And
if you've been
wounded and you
need a comrade
to pull you up?
So what?

Everything is
interwoven, and
the web is holy;
none of its parts
are unconnected.
They are composed
harmoniously,
and together they
compose the world.

What is divine deserves our respect because it is good;

What is human deserves our affection because it is like us.

The span we live is small—small as the corner of the earth in which we live it. Small as even the greatest renown, passed from mouth to mouth by short-lived stick figures, ignorant alike of themselves and those long dead.

Find fulfillment in what you're doing now, as Nature intended, and in superhuman truthfulness (every word, every utterance)—then your life will be happy. No one can prevent that.

In everything you do, even the smallest thing, remember the chain that links them. Nothing earthly succeeds by ignoring heaven, nothing heavenly by ignoring the earth.

Everything you
see will soon
alter and cease
to exist. Think
of how many
changes you've
already seen.

Choose not to
be harmed—
and you won't feel
harmed. Don't
feel harmed—and
you haven't been.

❖ ❖ ❖ ❖ ❖ ❖

LEAVE
OTHER
PEOPLE'S

MISTAKES WHERE THEY LIE.

❖ ❖ ❖ ❖ ❖ ❖

To the world:
Your harmony is
mine. Whatever
time you choose is
the right time.
Not late, not early.

To nature:
What the turn
of your seasons
brings me falls
like ripe fruit.

All things are
born from you,
exist in you,
return to you.

Something happens to you. Good. It was meant for you by nature, woven into the pattern from the beginning.

Each of us lives
only now, this
brief instant.
The rest has been
lived already, or is
impossible to see.

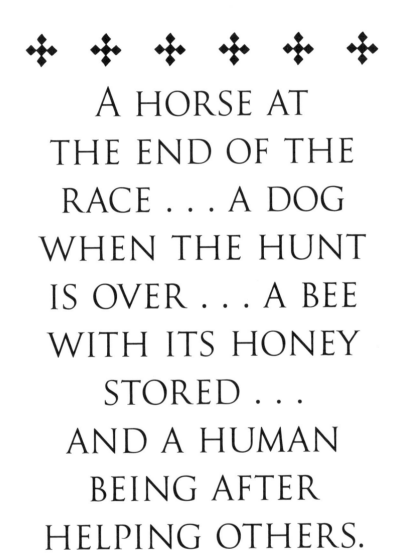

✤ ✤ ✤ ✤ ✤ ✤

A HORSE AT
THE END OF THE
RACE . . . A DOG
WHEN THE HUNT
IS OVER . . . A BEE
WITH ITS HONEY
STORED . . .
AND A HUMAN
BEING AFTER
HELPING OTHERS.

THEY DON'T
MAKE A FUSS
ABOUT IT. THEY
JUST GO ON
TO SOMETHING
ELSE, AS THE VINE
LOOKS FORWARD
TO BEARING
FRUIT AGAIN
IN SEASON.

Nothing pertains to human beings except what defines us as human. No other things can be demanded of us.

The things you think about determine the quality of your mind. Your soul takes on the color of your thoughts.

Anywhere you
can lead your
life, you can
lead a good one.

Things gravitate
toward what they
were intended for.

In a sense, people
are our proper
occupation. Our
job is to do them
good and put up
with them.

✦ ✦ ✦ ✦ ✦ ✦

THE IMPEDIMENT TO ACTION ADVANCES ACTION.

WHAT STANDS IN THE WAY BECOMES THE WAY.

✤ ✤ ✤ ✤ ✤ ✤

You can lead
an untroubled
life provided
you can grow,
can think and act
systematically.

So other people hurt me? That's their problem. Their character and actions are not mine.

_____

_____

_____

_____

_____

_____

_____

_____

_____

_____

_____

_____

_____

_____

_____

_____

_____

_____

_____

_____

_____

 Nothing belongs to you but your flesh and blood—and nothing else is under your control.

True good
fortune is what you
make for yourself.
Good fortune:
good character, good
intentions,
and good actions.

To move from one
unselfish action to
another with God
in mind. Only
there, delight and
stillness.

When jarred,
unavoidably, by
circumstances,
revert at once to
yourself, and
don't lose the
rhythm more
than you can help.

Pride is a master
of deception:
when you think
you're occupied
in the weightiest
business, that's
when he has
you in his spell.

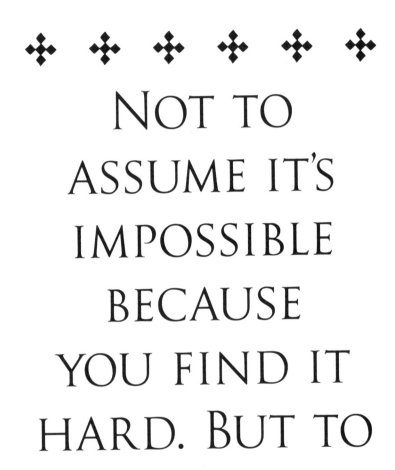

NOT TO
ASSUME IT'S
IMPOSSIBLE
BECAUSE
YOU FIND IT
HARD. BUT TO

RECOGNIZE THAT IF IT'S HUMANLY POSSIBLE, YOU CAN DO IT TOO.

❖ ❖ ❖ ❖ ❖ ❖

Nothing has
meaning to my
mind except its
own actions.
Which are within
its own control.

Does anything
genuinely beautiful need
supplementing? No more
than justice does—or truth,
or kindness, or humility.
Are any of those improved
by being praised?
Or damaged by contempt?
Is an emerald suddenly flawed
if no one admires it?

The lion's jaws,
the poisonous substances,
and every harmful thing—
from thorns to mud …
are by-products of the good
and beautiful. So don't look
at them as alien to what you
revere, but focus on the source
that all things spring from.

If we limited
"good" and "bad" to
our own actions,
we'd have no call
to challenge God,
or to treat other
people as enemies.

The only
thing that isn't
worthless: to
live this life out
truthfully and
rightly. And be
patient with
those who don't.

Nothing is as
encouraging as
when virtues are
visibly embodied
in the people
around us, when
we're practically
showered with
them. It's good to
keep this in mind.

Ambition means tying your well-being to what other people say or do. Self-indulgence means tying it to the things that happen to you. Sanity means tying it to your own actions.

Practice really hearing what people say.

Do your best to get inside their minds.

I can control
my thoughts as
necessary; then
how can I be
troubled? What is
outside my mind
means nothing
to it. Absorb that
lesson and your
feet stand firm.

A key point to bear in mind: The value of attentiveness varies in proportion to its object. You're better off not giving the small things more time than they deserve.

I have seen the beauty of good, and the ugliness of evil, and have recognized that the wrongdoer has a nature related to my own—not of the same blood or birth, but the same mind, and possessing a share of the divine.

Nothing that goes
on in anyone else's
mind can harm
you. Nor can the
shifts and changes
in the world
around you.

Remember this principle when something threatens to cause you pain: the thing itself was no misfortune at all; to endure it and prevail is great good fortune.

Don't you see how much you have to offer—beyond excuses like "can't"?

And yet you still settle for less.

Our own worth
is measured by
what we devote
our energy to.

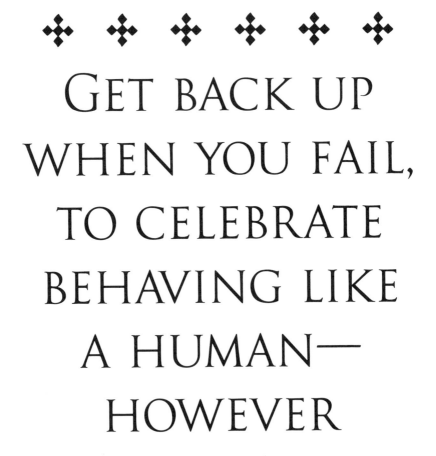

❖ ❖ ❖ ❖ ❖ ❖

GET BACK UP
WHEN YOU FAIL,
TO CELEBRATE
BEHAVING LIKE
A HUMAN—
HOWEVER

IMPERFECTLY—
AND FULLY
EMBRACE
THE PURSUIT
THAT YOU'VE
EMBARKED ON.

❖ ❖ ❖ ❖ ❖ ❖

Other people's
mistakes?
Leave them to
their makers.

To feel affection
for people even
when they make
mistakes is
uniquely human.

When people injure
you, ask yourself
what good or harm
they thought would
come of it. If you
understand that,
you'll feel sympathy
rather than outrage
or anger.

The mind's requirements are satisfied by doing what we should, and by the calm it brings us.

Don't pay attention to other people's minds.

Look straight ahead, where nature is leading you.

To love only what
happens, what
was destined. No
greater harmony.

Frightened of
change? But
what can exist
without it?

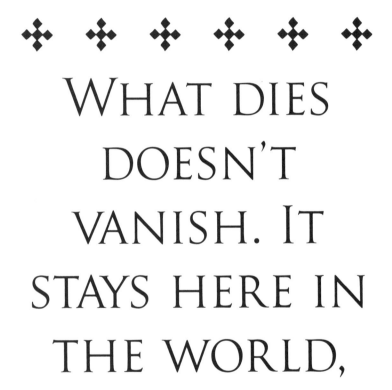

✢ ✢ ✢ ✢ ✢ ✢

WHAT DIES
DOESN'T
VANISH. IT
STAYS HERE IN
THE WORLD,

TRANSFORMED,
DISSOLVED, AS
PARTS OF THE
WORLD, AND
OF YOU.

✣ ✣ ✣ ✣ ✣ ✣

It's silly to
try to escape
other people's
faults. They are
inescapable. Just
try to escape
your own.

Joy for
humans
lies in
human
actions.

All our decisions,
urges, desires,
aversions lie
within. No evil
can touch them.

A rational being
can turn each
setback into raw
material and use it
to achieve its goal.

External things
are not the
problem. It's
your assessment
of them. Which
you can erase
right now.

People exist for one another.

You can instruct or endure them.

To do harm is to
do yourself harm.
To do an injustice
is to do yourself
an injustice—
it degrades you.

Indifference
to external
events. And a
commitment
to justice in
your own acts.

You can discard most of the junk that clutters your mind—things that exist only there—and clear out space for yourself.

HUMANS WERE
MADE TO HELP
OTHERS. AND
WHEN WE DO
HELP OTHERS—
OR HELP THEM TO

DO SOMETHING—
WE'RE DOING
WHAT WE WERE
DESIGNED FOR.
WE PERFORM
OUR FUNCTION.

❖ ❖ ❖ ❖ ❖ ❖

Whatever
happens to you
has been waiting
to happen since
the beginning
of time.

By keeping
in mind the
whole I form
a part of, I'll
accept whatever
happens.

When you wake up, ask yourself: Does it make any difference to you if other people blame you for doing what's right?

Stop talking
about what the
good man is like,
and just be one.

Each of us needs
what nature
gives us, when
nature gives it.

❖ ❖ ❖ ❖ ❖ ❖

Learn to ask of all actions, "Why are they

DOING
THAT?"
STARTING
WITH
YOUR OWN.

✤ ✤ ✤ ✤ ✤ ✤

Not just sound
judgments,
solid actions—
tolerance as well,
for those who try
to obstruct us or
give us trouble in
other ways.

Both are
deserters: the man
who breaks and
runs, and the one
who lets himself
be alienated
from his fellow
humans.

The soul as a sphere
in equilibrium:
Not grasping at
things beyond it or
retreating inward.
Not fragmenting
outward, not sinking
back on itself, but
ablaze with light and
looking at the truth,
without and within.

Someone
despises me.
That's their
problem. Mine:
not to do or
say anything
despicable.

As long as you do what's proper to your nature, and accept what the world's nature has in store—as long as you work for others' good, by any and all means—what is there that can harm you?

How much
more damage
anger and
grief do than
the things that
cause them.

Kindness is
invincible,
provided
it's sincere.

Pain is the opposite of strength, and so is anger. Both are things we suffer from, and yield to.

The student as boxer, not fencer. The fencer's weapon is picked up and put down again. The boxer's is part of him. All he has to do is clench his fist.

At all times, look at the thing itself—the thing behind the appearance—and unpack it by analysis.

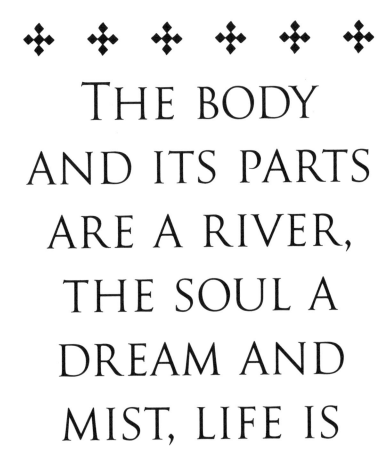

THE BODY
AND ITS PARTS
ARE A RIVER,
THE SOUL A
DREAM AND
MIST, LIFE IS

WARFARE AND
A JOURNEY
FAR FROM
HOME, LASTING
REPUTATION IS
OBLIVION.

✤ ✤ ✤ ✤ ✤ ✤

Whatever
happens has
always happened,
and always
will, and is
happening at this
very moment,
everywhere.

The present is all
we have to live in.
Or to lose.

Intelligence is
uniquely drawn
toward what is
akin to it, and
joins with it
inseparably, in
shared awareness.

The fraction of
infinity, of that
vast abyss of time,
allotted to each
of us. Absorbed
in an instant into
eternity.

People try to get
away from it all—
to the country, to
the beach, to the
mountains. You always
wish that you could
too. Which is idiotic:
you can get away from
it anytime you like.
By going within.

✣ ✣ ✣ ✣ ✣ ✣

WHAT DOESN'T TRANSMIT LIGHT

CREATES
ITS
OWN
DARKNESS.

❖ ❖ ❖ ❖ ❖ ❖

When you have trouble getting out of bed in the morning, remember that your defining characteristic—what defines a human being—is to work with others.

The mind without passions is a fortress.

No place is more secure.

The things
ordained for you—
teach yourself
to be at one with
those. And
the people who
share them with
you—treat them
with love.

Straight, not straightened.

It's quite possible
to be a good man
without anyone
realizing it.
Remember that.

Be like the rock that the waves keep crashing over.

It stands unmoved and the raging of the sea falls still around it.

ClarksonPotter.com
RandomHouseBooks.com

CLARKSON POTTER is a trademark and POTTER with colophon
is a registered trademark of Penguin Random House LLC.

ISBN 978-0-593-57997-8

Printed in the United States of America

Editor: Lindley Boegehold
Production editor: Sohayla Farman
Production manager: Luisa Francavilla
Copyeditor: Sarah Etinas
Book and cover design by: Danielle Deschenes

1st Printing

First Edition